A McGRAW-HILL NEW BIOLOGY

Scientific Adviser: Dr. Gwynne Vevers
Curator of the Aquarium and Invertebrates,
The Zoological Society of London

BIRDS OF PREY

THAT HUNT BY DAY

OTHER BOOKS IN THIS SERIES

Chimpanzees

Prue Napier
Illustrated by Douglas Bowness

Fishes

Gwynne Vevers
Illustrated by Alan Jessett

Frogs, Toads & Newts

F. D. Ommanney
Illustrated by Deborah Fulford

Spiders & Scorpions

J. L. Cloudsley-Thompson
Illustrated by Joyce Bee

Bees & Wasps

J. L. Cloudsley-Thompson
Illustrated by Joyce Bee

Crocodiles & Alligators

J. L. Cloudsley-Thompson
Illustrated by Joyce Bee

A McGRAW-HILL NEW BIOLOGY

Clive Catchpole

Birds of Prey
that hunt by day

Illustrated by David Nockels

McGRAW-HILL BOOK COMPANY

New York   St. Louis   San Francisco

Metric Conversion Table

1 centimeter = 0·39 inch
1 meter = 3·27 feet
1 kilometer = 0·62 mile

1 sq. centimeter = 0·15 sq. inch
1 sq. meter = 10·76 sq. feet
1 hectare = 2·47 acres
1 sq. kilometer = 0·39 sq. mile

1 kilogram = 2·21 lb (avoirdupois)
1 tonne = 0·98 (long) ton

Library of Congress Cataloging in Publication Data

Catchpole, Clive.
  Birds of prey that hunt by day.

  (A McGraw-Hill new biology)
  Includes index.
    SUMMARY: Investigates the lifestyle and breeding
behavior of vultures, secretary birds, hawks, buzzards,
eagles, kites, harriers, and falcons.
    1. Birds of prey—Juvenile literature. [1. Birds of prey]
I. Nockels, David. II. Title.
QL696.F3C36   598.9′1   76–43355
ISBN 0–07–010230–9 (lib. bdg.)

BIRDS OF PREY
that hunt by day

First distribution in the United States of America
by McGraw-Hill Book Company, 1977.
Text © Clive Catchpole 1975.
Illustrations © David Nockels 1975.
First printed in Great Britain for
The Bodley Head
by William Clowes & Sons Ltd., Beccles.
First published 1975

Contents

White-headed Vulture
(0·8 m.)

Imperial Eagle (0·8 m

Red Kite (0·6 m.)

Common Buzzard (0·5 m.)

Different types of birds of prey. The measurement
given for each bird is the approximate length in meters
from beak to tail, and the silhouette shows the
characteristic shape in flight.

1

Introduction

Birds, like fishes, amphibians, reptiles and mammals, belong to a group of animals which share an important characteristic: they all have a backbone. The backbone is made up of many small bones, called vertebrae, so we call these animals "vertebrates." Human beings are vertebrates, too, and you can easily feel the knobbly vertebrae which make up your backbone.

About two hundred million years ago there were no birds or mammals on the earth—only fishes, amphibians and reptiles. The reptiles for a time dominated the earth, and birds and mammals developed much later from reptile ancestors. Today, modern birds still show some signs of their reptile ancestry, such as their scaly feet and legs. Like most reptiles, birds lay eggs, but they have also developed important new characteristics which distinguish them from reptiles and in some ways make them more advanced. Like mammals, birds are "warm-blooded" which means they maintain a constant, high body temperature, even though the temperature of their surroundings may rise and fall. This means that in cold weather (or winter) birds can still be active and go about their normal daily lives,

Montagu's Harrier
(0·4 m.)

Gyr Falcon
(0·6 m.)

European
Sparrowhawk
(0·3 m.)

whereas amphibians and reptiles may become in-
active or even hibernate until the spring.

What makes birds really different from other
animals are their feathers, something that no other
animal group has. As well as forming a thick layer
over most of the body to protect them from the cold,
the large flight feathers on the wing give birds the
power to move in a way which man has always
envied. They can fly with effortless grace and without mechanical help, and of all the birds, some of the
most skillful and spectacular fliers are the birds of
prey.

8

What are birds of prey?

Any bird which preys upon other living animals for food could be called a bird of prey, but ornithologists use this description to identify only one group of birds which share two special characteristics.

First, most of them have very powerful, grasping feet with long, sharp talons. These are used in several ways: to kill the prey on impact by striking and piercing, to grip it tightly for carrying, and to hold it down while feeding. Secondly, they all possess large, hooked beaks, which are used to tear flesh from the dead prey while the feet hold it firmly down. The forelimbs or wings are used only for flying. They cannot help directly in killing or eating, and so the feet and beak have become highly specialized for these important tasks.

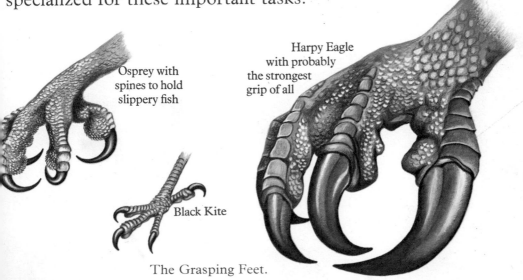

Osprey with spines to hold slippery fish

Harpy Eagle with probably the strongest grip of all

Black Kite

The Grasping Feet.

Peregrine Falcon

Egyptian Vulture

Golden Eagle

The Hooked Beaks.

Birds which have these special hooked beaks and powerful talons are called birds of prey, and there are two different groups of them. This book deals with the group that hunt by day and use mainly their eyes to find prey. Called the Falconiformes, this group contains the vultures, kites, buzzards, eagles, harriers and hawks, as well as the falcons. The other group (not dealt with here) contains the owls, called the Strigiformes. Owls hunt by night rather than by day, and although they do have special eyes to see in dim light, they rely mainly upon hearing to locate their prey.

3

Breeding behavior

Some birds of prey, such as the Golden Eagle in Scotland, live in the same place all year around. Others, such as the Osprey, leave their breeding area during the harsh winters of the north, and move south to warmer areas where food is more plentiful. This is called migration.

In spring the birds return to their breeding areas in the north and take up a territory. A territory is the name given to the piece of land which each breeding pair will nest in and jealously guard against all others of the same species. The males sometimes fight viciously to defend their territories, particularly near the nest, where no intruder will be allowed.

Birds of prey have some of the largest territories known. These usually stretch for many square miles because the territory must contain enough prey to feed a whole family of large birds for many months as well as a suitable place for nesting. Birds which do not migrate tend to stay in their territory for many years, and birds which do migrate still return each year to breed in the same territory.

Most birds of prey are very faithful, and once a bird has found a mate the pair will stay together for many years, until one of them dies. Before breeding begins, the pair will often display to each other. In a display the birds appear to "show off" to each other by performing exciting acrobatics while flying over the breeding area. The male Marsh Harrier appears to dive-bomb the female by flying at her at high speed, pulling away at the very last second, and even turning somersaults in the air. These extraordinary antics look almost as if the birds are celebrating their return to each other. But in all birds, displays are not just expressions of how they feel but also a kind of sign language. With various gestures and movements the birds are signaling to each other. The male is showing that he is ready to mate, and the female must show that she is ready to accept him. The breeding cycle can then begin.

Although displays take place in the air, the birds must come to the ground or perch on a tree for mating. The male hops onto the female's back, flapping his wings to keep his balance. In most birds, the male and female have similar external sex organs, and the two openings are pressed together. The male discharges sperm into the female very quickly and then hops off. The female will now be able to lay fertilized eggs, but in many cases a nest must first be built.

Not all birds of prey build a nest. The Andean Condor lays its single white egg on a bare, rocky ledge, high on a cliff or mountain. But most birds of

12

prey do build a nest, usually in a place safe from the reach of other predators. Eagles build their aeries on mountain ledges, or, as the Osprey does, high in the tree-tops. But sometimes there are no high places to nest in, and marshland birds such as the Marsh Harrier nest on the ground among the reeds.

Some tree-nesting birds, such as hobbies and kestrels, do not build their own nests. Instead they use the old nests of other birds, such as crows and magpies. The tiny African Pygmy Falcon always uses the nests of weaver birds, which are well protected as they are made of thorny sticks. But most build their own nests, usually a mass of sticks and twigs, sometimes lined with leaves or grass. In the European Sparrowhawk, the female builds a new nest each year, but in many species the male helps, too. Many eagles use the same nest again and again, adding to it year after year until it becomes an enormous structure. After being used for thirty-five years, one nest of the American Bald Eagle measured 3·6 meters by 2·4 meters. Eventually these huge nests may be blown down, which is not surprising as some of them must weigh over a tonne.

Birds of prey usually lay between one and six eggs every year. Most eagles' eggs are white, but many others, such as the Osprey's, are beautifully marked with a variety of colored blotches and speckles which help to camouflage them in the nest. The eggs are not round, but pointed at one end and

Marsh Harrier bringing food to young at nest on the ground.

rounded at the other, which makes them less likely to roll out of the nest or off a rocky ledge. In order to develop and hatch, the eggs must be kept as near body temperature as possible. This means that at least one of the parents, usually the female, must sit on the eggs continually to incubate them. In some species, such as the Bald Eagle, both sexes take turns to incubate the eggs while the other goes hunting for food. In others, such as the European Sparrowhawk, the female alone incubates through-out the thirty-five days of the incubation period until hatching. During this time, the female is fed on the nest by the male who is free to hunt. The male Marsh Harrier, returning from a hunt, calls his female from the nest and passes the prey to her in mid-air.

Eggs are usually laid several days apart, so one chick may hatch out before the rest. In eagles this

14

often happens, and in the Golden Eagle two chicks of different ages and sizes are frequently produced. What happens next is very strange. The older, larger eaglet starts to attack the younger one by violent wrestling and pecking. Eventually, the weaker eaglet dies. This occurs in many species of eagle, and although the reasons for it are not known, it seems a ruthless way of ensuring that only the very strongest survive. In most other birds of prey that lay several eggs, the young are raised together in a normal family group. While they are still young, the female continues to sit on them to keep them warm until their feathers have grown. This is called brooding. Food brought to the nest is torn up by the parents into small strips and given to the young birds. The young grow rapidly, and if only the male has been hunting, the female may need to join in to find enough food. The parents now spend less time preparing the food and may take off only some of

Golden Eagle at rocky aerie feeding two young eaglets.

Osprey at nest in the trees feeding fully-grown young.

the limbs or fur. Some birds of prey even swallow their prey whole, taking in large amounts of indigestible fur, feathers and bones. These are formed into a pellet in the gizzard and eventually regurgitated by special movements of the head and neck. By examining the many pellets found near the nest, it is possible to get some idea of what type of prey has been caught and eaten.

Eventually, the young become fully grown and it is time for them to leave the nest on the first flight. Before this, they will have practiced wing movements by hopping up and down on the edge of the nest, frantically flapping their wings and almost taking off. Suddenly, perhaps by accident, they are launched into the first real flight, which often ends quickly and with an awkward landing. Only by much practice will they learn how to fly and hunt as their parents can. Sometimes the parents will help by chasing, diving and twisting in the air, and even passing prey already caught. These games, like other examples of play in young animals, are really an important way of learning the complicated art of survival, for soon the young birds must leave their parents, and many of the young, weak and inexperienced will die in the first year. Some birds of prey live for over fifty years, and only a few are needed each year to maintain the population. Eventually, the few young that survive will find a territory of their own, attract a mate and breed themselves for the very first time.

4

Vultures and the Secretary Bird

Vultures are large birds of prey which soar in the air
They have large wide wings and a short tail. On the
ground they are somewhat ugly, usually with bald
heads and long, bare necks. Vultures are scavengers
which means that instead of hunting for live prey
they feed mainly on the carcasses of dead animals
Instead of flying fast, most vultures are slow and
weak, and really too large for efficient flapping

Vultures surround zebra carcass on an African plain.

light. Some of the common vultures of the East African plains, such as Ruppell's Griffon and the White-backed Vulture, are particularly weak and heavy after gorging on the carcass of a zebra or gazelle. If the birds are chased they will have to take off but will soon come to ground again. If this is repeated several times, they become exhausted and are easily caught by hand.

Vultures do not need to fly fast in order to catch living prey. Instead, they have developed ways of searching for dead prey by remaining high in the air for very long periods. Instead of using up energy in flapping flight, vultures (like gliders) soar effort-

A White-backed Vulture is on the left, a Lappet-faced
Vulture in the center and a Ruppell's Griffon
on the right.

lessly on outstretched wings in thermals. Air rises a
it warms, and thermals are upward currents of ai
heated by the hot ground below. By entering
thermal at the bottom and circling within it, a bir
can be carried hundreds of feet up, without usin
any energy. It will then soar and glide, continuall
searching the ground below for signs of prey. Whe
a carcass is sighted, the vulture goes into a long
steep glide towards it. A vulture can reach a carcas
five kilometers away in about six minutes, we
ahead of any scavenging hyenas on the ground
Other vultures further away may not see the carcas
themselves, but they see the gliding bird and soo
follow it. Others join in, and very soon a hundred c

Egyptian Vulture using a stone to break
open an ostrich egg.

Lammergeier dropping bone to break it open.
(Wing-span about 2·6 m.)

more hungry vultures may gather around the carcass.

One of the larger species, perhaps a Lappet-faced Vulture, will rip open the abdomen of the carcass with powerful strokes of its large, hooked beak. The biggest and fiercest birds now stick their heads into the carcass, pull out the entrails and eat them. This is why the larger vultures have bare heads and necks. They soon become covered in blood, and if they were feathered would afterwards be matted with dried blood and impossible to clean. When the larger vultures have become bloated with food, the smaller ones will move in and gradually strip the carcass bare.

The Egyptian Vulture is one of the smaller species which cleans up the bits and pieces and so

has a feathered neck and head. This bird is best known for its remarkable ability to use a primitive kind of tool to break open eggs of other birds such as ostriches. An egg may first be stolen from a nest and placed on the ground. A suitable stone is then selected and picked up in the beak. The bird approaches the egg and repeatedly throws the stone against the hard shell until the egg breaks. The egg is then eaten. This deliberate use of another object as a tool is a very advanced form of behavior found only in man and a few other animals.

Another remarkable vulture is the splendid Lammergeier, which resembles a falcon in flight. Its Spanish name, *quebrantahuesos*, literally means

Few California Condors, the largest birds in North America, are now left in the mountains of California. Their wing-span may be nearly 3 m.

bone-breaker. Being small, the Lammergeier is also forced to eat the remains of carcasses, and even eats the bones. Pieces of the skull, legs and horn from a Chamois have been found in a Lammergeier's stomach. Larger bones are picked up, and the bird flies high into the air before deliberately dropping them onto a large rock. The bones break open and the bird gouges out the marrow with a special hard tongue.

The American vultures include the largest birds of prey in the world, the condors. The Andean Condor from South America soars high over the Andes on wings nearly 3 meters across, and feeds on dead llamas, cattle and sheep. The California

23

Condor is similar, but only about fifty of these magnificent birds are now left and the species is in grave danger of extinction. Dead cattle, horses, deer and squirrels form the bulk of its diet, and poisoning of carcasses with strychnine to kill wolves and coyotes may have been one reason for its decline. Another is that when the settlers first came to California, the great soaring bird was an easy target for their guns. One of the most characteristic birds of the "Wild West" is certainly the "buzzard" or "John Crow." Not really a buzzard at all, this bird is the Turkey Vulture and, like the American Black Vulture, uses smell as well as sight to find dead prey. Alighting on the ground by a dead carcass, the Turkey Vulture approaches it stealthily, and having made sure it is dead skillfully pecks out the eyes and swallows them whole.

The Secretary Bird is so different from other birds of prey that it is placed in a separate group of its own. The name comes from the pen-like quills which appear to stick out from behind its ears. It lives in Africa and is unusual in that it has extremely long legs and hunts live prey on the ground. It stalks insects, lizards, snakes and rodents by stealthily walking over the grassy plains. It rushes towards the prey, and kills by stamping viciously with its powerful feet. Although it can fly it rarely does, and seems to prefer being on the ground.

Secretary Bird attacking python.
It stands about 1 m. high.

5

Kites and harriers

Black Kite in flight. (Wing-span about 1·5 m.)

Kites are fairly large birds of prey with angular wings and often a forked tail. Some, like vultures, are scavengers, but others hunt for a variety of living prey. Most kites lack the speed and agility of the hawks and falcons, and so take smaller, slower prey. The Black Kite is one of the most common and widespread birds of prey in the Old World, being found throughout Europe, Asia, Africa and Australia. In parts of Africa and Asia, Black Kites are important scavengers and they even nest and feed in towns. In other areas they hunt for a wide range of living prey, particularly small mammals and reptiles. In the sixteenth century the Red Kite of Europe was a common scavenger in the streets of London. It is now extremely rare in Britain and only a few pairs are left breeding in the mountains of Wales.

A number of kites feed on small invertebrate animals, and the Snail Kite is one of the most specialized of these. Found over much of South America, it extends north into Mexico and the Florida Everglades where it is known as the Everglade Kite. Hunting low over the marshes, it feeds entirely on freshwater snails. It has a long, hooked "winklepicker" beak, which is used to extract the snails without breaking their shell.

The Honey Buzzard of Europe and Asia is really a kite. Although it can take larger prey, as its name suggests, it attacks the nests of bees and wasps. The Honey Buzzard uses its strong feet to dig out the grubs, and its head has special, thick feathers to give some protection against being stung. But the most skillful and acrobatic of all the kites, the African Bat Hawk, is unusual among birds of prey. It hunts only at dusk and performs the difficult task of catching small bats on the wing. Equipped with very large,

Snail Kite feeding.

Honey Buzzard attacking bees' nest in a tree.

yellow eyes, it can see prey in very dark conditions. The Bat Hawk also has a large mouth, for after catching a bat with its talons, it then swallows the unfortunate creature whole, head first, and while still flying.

Harriers are rather slim birds of prey, with narrow, pointed wings and a long tail. They glide very low over open ground, and every few seconds flap to keep up their height. They quarter the ground, watching very closely, and as soon as they detect a small movement, pounce onto their un-suspecting prey. The Marsh Harrier is found over Europe, Asia, Africa, Australia and New Zealand, and as its name suggests, it prefers to nest and hunt in marshy areas. It may take frogs and small duck-lings, as well as small mammals. The Marsh Hawk, too, is found in Europe and Asia, but also in North America. Small mammals such as mice and voles are taken, and the Marsh Hawk may detect them by the rustlings and squeaks they make as well as by sight.

Marsh Hawk drops onto a vole.
(Wing-span about 1 m.)

6

Hawks and buzzards

The true hawks are quite small birds of prey, but very skillful in the air. They have short, rounded wings and long tails which make them very maneuverable in flight. Hawks lack stamina for long flights over open country, and instead hunt mainly in woodland, or fly low over bushes and hedges. They rely on surprise and speed over short distances to catch other birds in the air. The European Sparrowhawk takes all kinds of birds, from tiny wrens and tits to pigeons and young game birds. Persecution by

European Sparrowhawk chasing Blue Tit.
(Wing-span about 0·7 m.)

Northern Rough-legged Buzzard
soaring.
(Wing-span about 1·4 m.)

gamekeepers and poisoning by pesticides have made
this species very rare in Britain now. The African
Little Sparrow Hawk is only the size of a Starling,
and hawks for large insects such as dragonflies and
butterflies, as well as small birds.

The Northern Goshawk is the largest hawk, and
probably the fiercest, too. It is found in North
America as well as Europe, Asia and Japan, and
usually inhabits coniferous forest. The Northern
Goshawk can take larger birds, such as pheasants,
ducks and grebes, as well as small mammals like
lemmings. Although the kill is usually swift, this
fierce hawk will often continue to fight on the ground
and is sometimes dragged along by larger prey.

Hawks can often be seen following flocks of
smaller birds, hoping to pick off a straggler. The
Sharp-shinned Hawk of North America is often
seen in large numbers on autumn migration,
following the migrating flocks of smaller birds.

31

Red-tailed Hawk in flight. (Wing-span about 1·2 m.)

Buzzards are larger, bulky birds of prey, with broad wings and short, rounded tails. When circling high in the sky they resemble small eagles but have less prominent heads and beaks. Buzzards use a variety of hunting techniques. Many soar or hover in the air and others fly low like harriers. Some may still hunt from a perch or even walk on the ground when hunting. The Common Buzzard is found over most of Europe, and although it has a wing span of some 1·2 meters feeds on a variety of small animals. Small mammals, birds, reptiles, amphibians and fish may be taken, and even invertebrates such as earthworms and beetles. The Common Buzzard is even a scavenger at times. The Northern Rough-legged Buzzard is found further north in both North America and Europe, and extends into the cold, Arctic tundra. It feeds mainly on lemmings, and greatly increases its numbers after a good lemming year.

Many of the American "hawks," such as the Red-shouldered Hawk and the Broad-winged Hawk, are really buzzards. The Red-tailed Hawk is a large buzzard, and feeds on mammals such as rats, rabbits and even the North American opossum. The Galapagos Hawk, like many animals in the Galapagos Islands, is extremely tame. It feeds mainly on the many reptiles of the Galapagos, such as lizards, snakes, tortoises, turtles and even small iguanas.

Osprey carrying fish.
(Wing-span about 1·4 m.)

7

Eagles and the Osprey

Eagles are very large birds of prey which soar majestically on long, broad wings, and have prominent beaks and heads. The wingspan of the largest eagles may be over 2·4 meters. About one quarter of all birds of prey are eagles, and they can be divided into four main groups. The largest group are the true or booted eagles, so-called because they have feathers on their legs right down to their toes. The other groups are the fish and sea eagles, the snake eagles, and the harpy eagles. Because of their great size eagles often hunt for very large prey.

Fish eagles are smaller than sea eagles, and hunt mainly for fish in rivers and freshwater lakes. The Lesser Fishing Eagle of India, Burma and Malaya swoops down and snatches fish from the water. Under the toes are tiny spikes which give a firm grip on such slippery prey. The Osprey is even better equipped for catching fish. As well as having spikes under the toes and needle-sharp claws, the Osprey has two talons at the front of the foot and two at the back, to give an even better grip. When flying over the water and seeing a fish, the Osprey does not snatch at it, but drops down onto its feet first. It often enters the water with a great splash, but has

White-tailed Sea Eagle soaring over the open sea.
(Wing-span about 2·5 m.)

special waterproof feathers. The grip is so firm that some Ospreys have been unable to let go of a really large fish and have been dragged under and drowned. Large fish have been caught by fishermen with the skeleton of an Osprey still clinging to the back.

Sea eagles are much larger and hunt over the sea as well as rivers and lakes. The White-tailed Sea Eagle is found over much of Europe and Asia, as well as Greenland and Iceland. In the eighteenth century it was common in Britain but due to persecution by gamekeepers and shepherds has long since vanished. Although a few did take small lambs, they mainly scavenged on the carcasses of dead sheep, and normally catch large seafish such as cod and halibut. Seabirds such as Shags and Puffins are taken, too, and mammals such as lemmings, hares and small

Bald Eagle with salmon;
Serpent Eagle with snake.

deer. There are even records of a White-tailed Sea Eagle attacking seals in the sea.

The national emblem of the United States of America is the Bald Eagle which ranges from Alaska to Florida. This handsome bird mainly scavenges on dead salmon and other fish, but, because of its fondness for salmon in traps and valuable furry mammals, over a hundred thousand birds have been shot. The slaughter was halted in 1940, to save the national bird from extinction.

Snake eagles have short, strong toes which are used to grasp and kill snakes and lizards. They rely on skill and speed to catch and immobilize snakes quickly before they can be bitten. Although snake eagles do have thick scales on their legs to give some protection, they are not immune to snake venoms and can die from snakebite. The Short-toed or Serpent Eagle is found in southern Europe, central Asia and Africa. Hovering or gliding in the air, as soon as it spots a snake on the ground it plunges down and quickly snatches it up. The wriggling snake is threaded through the talons until the head is reached. It is then crushed by the powerful talons or even torn off. The snake is then swallowed whole while the eagle is still in flight. Larger snakes may be taken to a favorite perch and eaten later. As many as a thousand snakes may be needed to feed a family of Serpent Eagles in one year.

Harpy Eagle.

Harpy eagles are large, forest-dwelling eagles from South America, the Philippines and New Guinea. The Harpy Eagle is the largest eagle of all, and certainly the most powerful, with enormous talons. In the Amazon jungle of South America it hunts and kills large mammals such as sloths, peccaries and monkeys. The Monkey-eating Eagle of the Philippines is now the rarest eagle in the world, with not more than fifty pairs left. Enormously powerful like the Harpy, it does kill monkeys but will also take flying squirrels and large forest birds such as hornbills.

The true or "booted" eagles are the largest and most widespread group of eagles. Magnificent, large, soaring birds, they hunt for a wide variety of prey, including larger, fast-moving mammals. Stories that

Golden Eagle attacking rabbit. (Wing-span about 2 m.)

they also snatch human babies are not true, but young mammals such as lambs are always in danger of being carried off. The Tawny Eagle is the most numerous eagle in the world, and is found over much of Europe, Asia and Africa. Soaring over the open steppes and plains, it swoops down on small mammals such as hares, rats and wolves. The larger Golden Eagle is also found in Europe, Asia and Africa, but is the only true eagle which occurs in North America. Prey is generally about the size of a hare, but the Siberian Golden Eagle may take larger prey such as deer, foxes and wolves.

The Wedge-tailed Eagle of Australia used to feed on wallabies, bandicoots and a variety of larger birds and lizards. It developed a taste for young lambs when sheep were introduced into Australia and as a result has been persecuted by sheep farmers ever since. As there are no vultures in Australia, the Wedge-tailed Eagle is the most important scavenger and soars like a vulture as well as swooping to attack live prey.

The Crowned Eagle is perhaps the most beautiful as well as the most powerful of the African eagles. Hunting low through the forest, it can take very large prey such as bushbuck and antelope up to fourteen kilograms. Even the Crowned Eagle cannot lift such a weight, so it dismantles the carcass. Like the leopard it then hides pieces of meat in trees for eating later.

8

Falcons and falconry

Falcons are in many ways the most advanced of all the birds of prey. They have long, pointed wings and long tails, and they fly very fast with unequaled skill. This enables them to pursue, catch and kill fast-flying birds in the air. Many falcons kill by the sheer speed and force of a powerful dive onto the prey, called "stooping."

Falcons are unusual in that they build no nests of their own. They either lay eggs in no nest at all, or use old nests of other birds.

Pygmy falcons are not much bigger than a sparrow, but can kill other birds twice their size. They hunt through woodland like sparrowhawks, in short dashes rather than with long stoops like the bigger falcons. The Red-legged Falconet from India and Vietnam is the smallest, and takes mainly large insects as well as birds. The African Pygmy Falcon is similar, but will also take small mammals.

Kestrels are found in most parts of the world, and the Common Kestrel is the most common bird of prey in Europe. It can occupy almost any habitat, and is even found nesting on buildings in large cities. It has developed a special hunting technique, hovering perfectly still in the air with rapidly beating wings. Watching the ground it dives down onto any small animal seen moving. Small mammals, such as voles and mice are its main prey, but birds, reptiles, insects and even earthworms are also taken.

The Pigeon Hawk is found in Europe, Asia and

Common Kestrel
hovering (0·3 m.)

European Hobby (0·3 m.)

Red-legged Falconet
(0·15 m.)

A variety of falcons. The measurement given for each
bird is the approximate length in meters
from beak to tail.

North America. It hunts fast and low over open country and makes short stoops to take a variety of birds.

Hobbies are fast, dashing hunters in the air. The European Hobby is fast enough to catch bats and swifts, and skimming through the air its streamlined shape even resembles a large swift.

The Peregrine Falcon is perhaps the most successful falcon, being found almost everywhere in the world except the Arctic. It is so fast and agile that it can pursue and catch small, fast birds such as swallows as well as larger game birds. When stooping, it closes its wings and hurtles down at speeds of up to two hundred miles an hour. It strikes the prey with such force that even a large pheasant may be dashed to the ground dead, leaving only a cloud of feathers in the air.

The art of falconry has been practiced for thousands of years in many parts of the world. Although often considered to be a sport, it may well have started as a way of using birds of prey to catch food for man. Falcons are commonly used, but so are hawks and, occasionally, eagles. Falconers are wise to select a species which is best suited to hunt in their particular area. In woodland sparrowhawks and goshawks are best, and in open country falcons or eagles.

Young birds are more easily trained, but training takes a long time and needs much care and patience.

Peregrine Falcon attacking pheasant.
(Wing-span about 1 m.)

A special leather hood is made to fit each bird
individually. When the eyes are covered, a bird will
remain calm and quiet. Leather straps, called jesses,
attach the legs to a perch, and small bells on the legs
help to find it when lost or escaped. The bird is first

trained to sit on the falconer's gloved hand and feed, and later to return to the glove. It is trained to drop onto a lure pulled along on a lead. The lure is then swung in the air, and the bird learns to chase and catch it. Eventually, after months of practice, the bird is flown at real prey and learns to kill for the very first time.

Large falcons, such as the Peregrine, Lanner and Saker, are often used against game birds such as pheasants, partridge and quail. Arabs use the Saker to hunt large bustards and even gazelles. The Saker only slows the gazelle down, and packs of trained dogs are used to complete the kill. In India goshawks are also used with dogs. Here the dog flushes out partridges and quail, and the goshawk is flung straight at them with a quick movement of the falconer's arm. In Mongolia, eagles are used to catch more spectacular prey. Golden Eagles are used against foxes and wolves for their valuable skins, and Bonelli's Eagles to hunt gazelles.

Falcon wearing decorated hood.

Index